RICKY MARTIN

RICKY MARTIN

KATHIE BERGQUIST

THE UNOFFICIAL · BOOK ·

BILLBOARD BOOKS

First published in 1999 by
Virgin Books
An imprint of
Virgin Publishing Ltd
Thames Wharf Studios
Rainville Road
London
W6 9HT

First published in the United States in 1999 by Billboard Books, a division of
Watson-Guptill Publications, an imprint of BPI Communications Inc., at 1515
Broadway, New York, NY 10036.

Library of Congress Cataloging-in-Publication Data for this title can be
obtained from the Library of Congress.
Library of Congress Catalog Card Number: 99-90680
ISBN 0 8230 8407 8

Printed and bound by Butler & Tanner Ltd

Designed by Stonecastle Graphics Ltd

First printing 1999

1 2 3 4 5 6 7 8 9/06 05 04 03 02 01 00 99

Contents

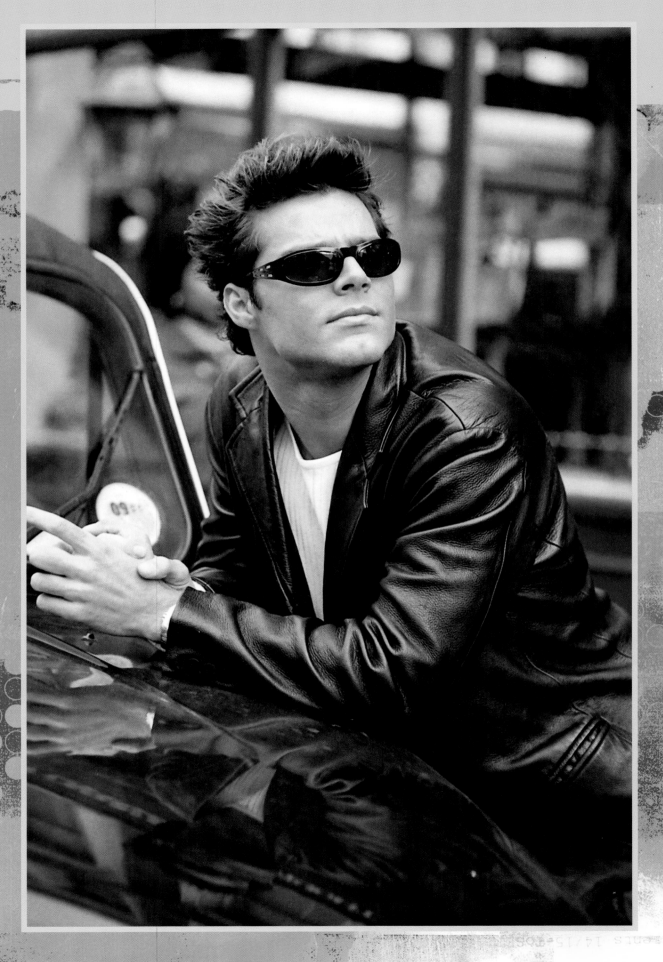

Chapter One
¡La Vida Ricky!

Ricky Martin is hot! After a show-stopping performance at the American Grammy Awards in early 1999, the dashing superstar's self-titled CD, his debut English language release, became a record-breaking triumph. His Grammy performance also presented Ricky to billions of television viewers, including 26 million American households, and it was love at first sight.

RICKY MARTIN sold 661,000 copies in its first week in the stores, and went on to be awarded triple-Platinum status (three million copies) in its first month of release. It became the best-selling debut album ever by a Hispanic artist in the US *Billboard* charts.

But this incredible success was just another chapter in Ricky's amazing career. His millions of new American fans were just catching on to what the rest of the world already knew: Ricky Martin is a musical phenomenon!

It all started humbly enough, with what Ricky describes as a perfectly normal childhood in suburban San Juan, Puerto Rico. From the start, Ricky loved the spotlight and jumped at every opportunity he had to perform. He took acting and dance lessons and appeared in television commercials. His "normal" childhood quickly came to an end in 1983, however, when he joined Latin teen pop sensation Menudo.

Ricky loved the spotlight and jumped at every opportunity he had to perform.

Over the next five years, Ricky would experience the joy of performing in front of vast crowds and the adulation of millions. According to Ricky his time with the group was the best education he could have had to prepare him for his future as a solo artist.

Menudo was just the beginning of a remarkably diverse and accomplished career. From daytime TV idol to the Broadway stage, and throughout his record-breaking solo recording career, Ricky's impact has been nothing less than spectacular.

Menudo was just the beginning of a remarkably diverse and accomplished career.

Ricky has so far released four solo albums each one more successful than the last. His third, *A Medio Vivir*, included the smash hit "(Uno Dos Tres) Maria", which remained in the Latin charts throughout the world for two years!

Parallel to his musical exploits, Ricky also built a solid acting career in Latin America, and earned a Heraldo award (the Mexican equivalent of an Oscar) to show for it.

Ricky's career reached new heights when he was asked to perform the theme song for the 1998 soccer World Cup in France. His performance was beamed live to two billion soccer fans worldwide, and "La Copa de la Vida" shot to number one in 22 countries around the world. It was Ricky's biggest hit to date.

His fourth album, *Vuelve*, sold more than six million copies worldwide, staking out a seemingly permanent position at the top of *Billboard*'s Latin chart. This album also earned Ricky his first Grammy Award for best Latin Pop Record, and two *Billboard* awards.

Today the devotion of Ricky's millions of fans worldwide can only be compared to Beatlemania. Huge crowds gather at every appearance he makes. Throngs of crying, screaming fans wait for hours just for a glimpse of Ricky. Thousands of web pages are devoted to him. And the first single to be released from *Ricky Martin*, "Livin' La Vida Loca", is on constant rotation on radios around the world.

Just what is it about this sexy superstar that drives millions of people crazy with Ricky fever? It could be his movie star looks – piercing dark eyes, chiselled features and a wicked smile. Or it could be his hip-swivelling sexy dance moves, burning up stages wherever he performs. Whatever the physical attractions, Ricky's appeal has always been more than just skin-deep. He has a certain quality that appeals to everyone: women and men, young and old. He has a refreshingly positive attitude and wholesome image. And with his charm, humility, looks, style and remarkable talent, Ricky is definitely the kind of guy that you'd want to bring home to mother!

Throngs of crying, screaming fans wait for hours just for a glimpse of Ricky.

Chapter Two
Little Ricky

Ricky Martin was born in Hato Rey, Puerto Rico on 24 December 1971, an early Christmas present for his parents Nereida Morales and Enrique Negroni. The only child of Nereida and Enrique, their little son was named Enrique Martin Morales.

P UERTO RICO, the birthplace of Salsa, is an island that is crazy about music. With a population of about four million, it boasts over 100 radio stations. Music was important to Ricky from the start, although his earliest musical tastes were largely influenced by his older brothers and leaned more in the direction of American rock music than traditional Latin tunes. The first record he bought was by David Bowie, and he also enjoyed rock groups like Cheap Trick, Boston and Journey. At the time, it wasn't cool in Puerto Rico for kids to be into Latin music.

One day Ricky's mother, sick of listening to her son's rock music, introduced him to the Latin sound by taking him to see Salsa legends Celia Cruz and Tito Puente. Even though he admits that he was a little bored at the time, Ricky is grateful to his mother for opening his eyes to his cultural heritage. It was a defining moment in his musical career; from that moment on he felt proud of who he was and where he was from.

Ricky is grateful to his mother for opening his eyes to his cultural heritage.

From the moment he learned to talk, Ricky always wanted to be in the spotlight. At the age of six, Ricky told his father that he wanted to be a performer, and his father immediately asked what he could do to help him. Since then his parents have been very supportive of Ricky's ambitions, teaching him to be stubborn and to believe in himself. Soon little Ricky was enrolled in acting and dancing lessons and began appearing in television commercials, including ads for Burger King and Orange Crush. In school he sang in the choir and acted in plays.

When Ricky was ten years old he became aware of a new sensation in Latin music: Menudo. This all-boy pop group had an ever-changing lineup of teenage members, who had to leave the group when they reached the age of 17. For the first time in his life, Ricky set his sights on a concrete goal: more than anything he wanted to be a member of Menudo.

At first, Ricky's interest in Menudo had little to do with singing and music. What attracted him was the chance to take to the stage and perform before adoring fans. Fame, fortune and a once-in-a-lifetime opportunity to see the world – what ten-year-old with stars in his eyes wouldn't jump at the chance?

But fame didn't come easily for Ricky. He was turned down for the group twice – both times for being too young and too small. But when Ricky reached the age of twelve, as luck would have it the group's manager was again looking around for a talented teenager to replace Ricky Melendez, who was getting too old to be in the group. It was Ricky's big break!

Ricky made an immediate impression with Menudo fans. The youngest and smallest member of the group, he was immediately dubbed Little Ricky, Ricky II and Kiki (which was also his father's nickname for him). Soon Ricky was performing in sold-out concerts on every continent. It was a dream come true. Fans watched Little Ricky grow up right before their eyes, and during what became Menudo's most successful period Little Ricky quickly became one of the group's brightest stars.

From the moment he learned to talk, Ricky always wanted to be in the spotlight.

Despite their success, being in Menudo was not always easy for Ricky and the other members of the group. During his formative years, he couldn't make such simple decisions as who to talk to and where to go without getting permission from his manager. His clothes were chosen for him. His performance schedules were rigorous and he had little control over his life. He was part of a product and had to conform to its standards. He has said that while he was growing up he felt as if the hotel room was his school and the hotel lobby was his playground.

In addition, he had to move away from home to be with the band full time. His absence caused a serious rift between Ricky and his (by now divorced) parents, who were jealously possessive of him. It was difficult for him to divide his time between each of them, and they both wanted to see him more. As a result, Ricky had a huge falling out with his father and had his name legally changed from Enrique Morales to Ricky Martin. His father stopped talking to him and it was ten years before they reconciled.

None of these hardships ruined Ricky's spirit, however. He has credited his years in Menudo with giving him the confidence to reach for his dreams, teaching him the discipline a performing career requires, and offering him opportunities he might have never had if it wasn't for Menudo. The group also

At his last performance he cried and cried.

introduced Ricky to Robi Rosa, a fellow member, who would later become a key part of Ricky's solo success.

The Menudo chapter in Ricky's life ended when the young heartthrob was 17 and it was his turn to be replaced. At his last performance he cried and cried. Then, free of the group after five years, he returned to Puerto Rico to finish his education. Deciding he needed some time to himself, he moved to New York, unsure of what the future held. He has said that the year he spent bumming around in New York was one of the best years of his life, because he was able to figure out who he was, what he wanted, and what was important to him. At 18, he was determined that his best years were still ahead of him. He was right.

Menudo Mania

ALMOST TWENTY years before Backstreet Boys, 'N Sync and 98°, another all-boy supergroup was breaking records and hearts all over the world. Their name was Menudo.

In 1977, Edgardo Diaz came up with an exciting new concept. Suppose someone put together an all-boy teen group, whose members were rotated out when they reached a certain age, so the group would always be young? After holding auditions to find the right guys, Diaz formed Menudo (which, besides being tripe soup, essentially translates to "small change").

The original members were two sets of brothers: Nefty and Fernando Sallaberry and Carlos, Oscar and Ricky Melendez. Ricky Melendez, who was the youngest to join the group at the age of eight, was a member of Menudo for seven years.

In 1978, Menudo's first appearance in New York caused chaos as hordes of screaming girls and women went crazy for the young hunks. As a result of their increasing fame, Menudo starred in TV specials throughout Latin America. Their international appeal grew and the group recorded albums in five languages: English, Spanish, Portuguese, Tagalog (Philippine) and Italian.

In 1978, Menudo's first appearance in New York caused chaos as hordes of screaming girls and women went crazy for the young hunks.

In 1983, the year that Ricky Martin joined the group, Menudo set a world record by playing to the largest audience ever.

Youth Ambassadors for Unicef. In addition to spreading goodwill in the name of peace, the group also became involved with anti-drug and stay-in-school campaigns.

For the group's tenth anniversary in 1987, the boys played to sold-out houses throughout Latin America and the Philippines. And in 1988, 2,000 screaming fans stormed security at a shopping mall appearance in San Antonio, Texas and began tearing the clothes off the guys, prompting the media to dub the craze "Spanish Beatlemania"!

Since their inception, Menudo has recorded 31 albums and clocked up total sales surpassing 20 million. In 1999, The group designed by Edgardo Diaz more than 20 years ago is still touring and recording. Their current line-up includes Abel Talamantez, Andres Blasquez, Edgar Anthony Galindo, Alexis Grullon and Didier Hernandez.

In 1983, the year that Ricky Martin joined the group, Menudo set a world record by playing to the largest audience ever. Their performance in front of 105,000 fans packed into the Azteca stadium in Mexico City was recorded in *The Guinness Book of Records*.

In 1984, the United Nations appointed Menudo as International

Chapter Three
Ricky's Music

Ricky Martin has always said that the secret of his phenomenal musical success is his experimentation with different musical cultures. Pop and rock merge seamlessly with a variety of Latin influences, and techno meets flamenco guitar and Brazilian rumba, combining to form an international celebration of music.

RICKY CITES his musical influences as David Bowie, Paul Simon, Sting and Julio Iglesias, all performers who have not been afraid to combine traditional musical elements from around the world to give them a contemporary edge.

Ricky released his first solo album, *Ricky Martin*, in 1992, while he was starring in the Mexican soap opera *Alcazar*

Una Estrella II. It was such a success that he was soon rushed back into the studio by his label, Sony Discos, to record a follow-up, *Me Amaras*, which was released in 1993. Both albums were catchy and fun, appealing to his fans from the Menudo days as well as growing group of new admirers.

In 1995, the release of his third album, *A Medio Vivir* marked a turning point in Ricky's musical career. It was produced by KC Porter (who has worked with Patti LaBelle and Richard Marx) and, for the first time, Ricky's former Menudo colleague Robi Rosa. Since the days of Menudo, Rosa had become a performer, producer and songwriter in his own right, and Ricky had long believed that his old colleague was a musical genius.

In 1995, the release of his third album, A Medio Vivir, marked a turning point in Ricky's musical career.

The collaboration between Ricky and Robi brought a rockier approach to Ricky's Latin styling that would catapult Ricky to new heights of success. The single "(Uno Dos Tres) Maria" sold four million copies around the world and was in constant radio rotation, while international sales of *A Medio Vivir* reached 600,000 in its first six months of release. Ricky toured constantly, and although he sang in Spanish he made fans in every country he visited.

Thanks to his booming international fame, Ricky was then asked to record and perform the theme song for the 1998 soccer World Cup in France. On "La Copa de la Vida" (The Cup of Life) he collaborated with

Ricky toured constantly, and although he sang in Spanish he made fans in every country he visited.

acclaimed producer Desmond Child, famed for his work with Aerosmith and Bon Jovi. During the opening ceremony Ricky performed "La Copa de la Vida" on live television, reaching over a billion viewers. Ricky's electric performance and the song's exciting rhythms catapulted the song to number one in 22 countries around the world.

Ricky featured "La Copa de la Vida" on his 1998 release, the best-selling *Vuelve*. Encouraged by the success of "La Copa de la Vida", he also chose to continue his successful collaboration with Desmond Child. The result was a remarkable album which went Platinum in 20 countries, selling an enormous 1.7 million copies in the US alone! It staked out a near-permanent position on the *Billboard* Latin charts, and also made a distinguished appearance on the *Billboard* Top 100. Ricky toured extensively to promote the album, playing sold-out concerts in Latin America, Europe, Asia and Australia.

The international success of *Vuelve* culminated when Ricky was nominated for a 1999 Grammy award for Best Latin Pop Record, and was invited to perform his hit song live at the televised ceremony. He has said that he was more excited about being asked to perform than he was about his nomination! He would be strutting his stuff, not just in front of some of the biggest and most legendary names in the music industry, but also for billions of TV viewers around the world!

Backstage before his performance at the Grammys, Ricky was nervous. He was about to perform in front of people he had idolized for years – Sting, Madonna, even Luciano Pavarotti! He calmed down by giving himself a pep talk, telling himself just to go out there and enjoy himself.

The pep talk worked. Two hours into an otherwise typical

awards ceremony, Ricky exploded on to the stage and electrified the audience. Surrounded by stilt walkers and Latin drummers, Ricky brought the house down with "La Copa de la Vida". The auditorium came alive as the audience got to their feet dancing and cheering, and at the end applauded Ricky with a standing ovation. In living rooms all over the world, people were asking themselves, "Who *is* this guy?"

Ricky will surely never forget that night. In addition to his show-stopping performance, he went on to win the award for Best Latin Pop Record for *Vuelve*. In his acceptance speech, an elated Ricky gushed thanks to many of the people who had helped him achieve such success, including Robi Rosa, KC Porter and Sony Music. The passion and vitality of Latin music had finally been recognized with an award for its biggest star.

> He was about to perform in front of people he had idolized for years – Sting, Madonna, even Luciano Pavarotti!

Over two years in the making, Ricky's self-titled English language debut was released on 11 May 1999. While his label, Columbia's C2 Records, was in a hurry to get it out (they rushed it into stores two weeks ahead of schedule to capitalize on Ricky's show-stopping Grammy performance), Ricky was in no hurry to record it. He wanted to make sure that his first album in English was something he'd always be proud of, so he spent time working with some of the most successful producers in the pop music industry, including Emilio Estefan, producer and husband of Gloria Estefan, and William Orbit, who produced Madonna's *Ray of Light* album.

While *Ricky Martin* was Ricky's debut in English, it was not the first time that he had recorded in a language other than Spanish. Recording in other languages is important for Ricky as a communicator. His ambition is to introduce himself and his music to the world, and if that means speaking another language, he's happy to do it. And after Ricky's triumph at the Grammys, the timing was definitely right to tackle the huge English language market. Ricky emphasizes, however, that he will never stop singing in Spanish, his mother tongue.

The first single to be released from *Ricky Martin* was the smash hit "Livin' La Vida Loca". With its irresistible Brazilian rhythms, a driving horn section and a classic

> # He wanted to make sure that his first album in English was something he'd always be proud of.

1960s bassline-style, "Livin' La Vida Loca" became the biggest-selling US number one single in the history of Columbia records!

Besides "Livin' La Vida Loca," the most talked-about cut on *Ricky Martin* was a last-minute addition – a duet with Madonna. Written and produced by Madonna and William Orbit, "Be Careful (Cuidado Con Mi Corazón)" mixes ambient electronica with flamenco guitar and features vocals in both Spanish and English. The duet came about after the pair met at the Grammy awards. Despite stories of tension in the recording studio, Ricky has said that Madonna taught him how to be more efficient and that she is "an amazing human being".

The album also includes "Spanglish" versions of two previously released hits: "La Copa de la Vida" and "(Uno Dos Tres) Maria", sung in a combination of English and Spanish. Of all the songs on *Ricky Martin*, Ricky particularly loves "I Am Made of You". He says that the song is a "conversation with a higher power" and reflects his state of mind right now.

Ricky Martin achieved its goal of bringing Ricky's music to a wider audience – and more! In its first week of release in the US, the CD sold over 600,000 copies, smashing straight in at number one. It is, he says, the best album he has ever recorded. He has revealed that the message of the album is to be who you are and not be afraid to express yourself. Ricky's amazing music career is proof of this remarkable guy's formula for success.

Ricky has said that Madonna taught him how to be more efficient and that she is "an amazing human being".

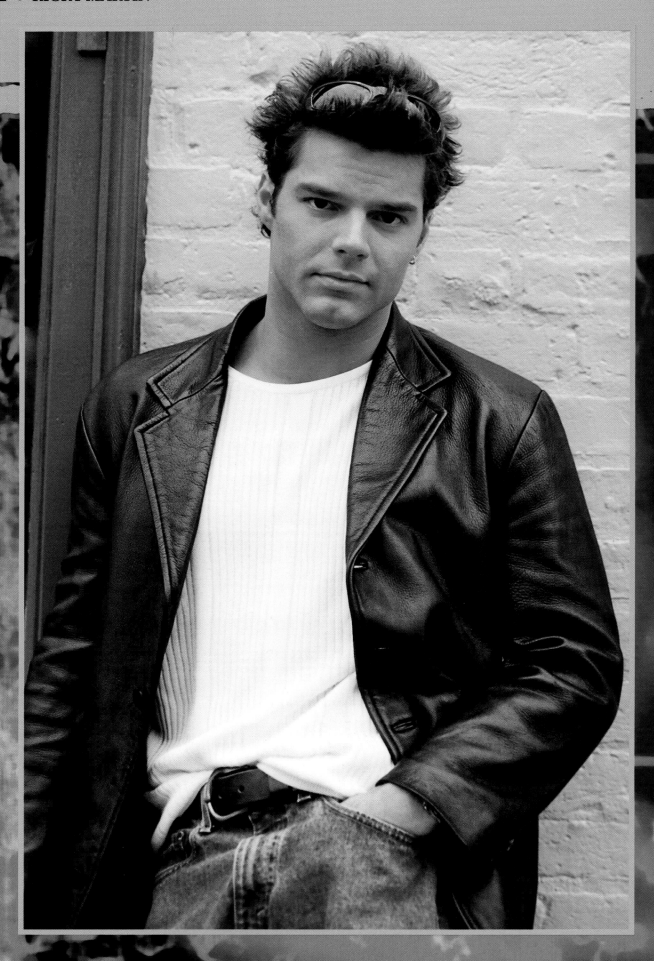

Chapter Four
Stage and Screen

As a child, Ricky was more interested in an acting career than a musical career. As luck would have it, he would have the opportunity to explore both options – each one with great success!

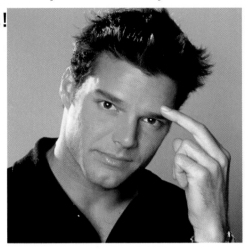

RICKY HAD his first taste of life in front of the camera when he was very young, acting in commercials and school plays from the age of seven. Then, when he was a member of Menudo, Ricky had another chance to show off his acting skills when the band made a guest appearance on the American television show *Love Boat*.

While Ricky was in New York in 1990, trying to decide what to do next with his life after he had left Menudo, he received a phonecall offering him a role in a musical in Mexico, *Mama Ama El Rock 'n' Roll*. Not wanting to appear desperate, Ricky put his hand over the mouthpiece while he jumped up and down with joy. Then he got back on the phone and stated calmly that he was interested.

While acting in Mexico, Ricky received another opportunity. He was offered the part of Pablo in a Mexican soap opera called *Alcazar Una Estrella II*, which he eagerly took up. Pablo was a musician in a band called Munecos de Papel, which actually did a real-life concert tour of Mexico with all the band members playing their roles from the soap!

Alcazar Una Estrella II was such a big show that it was turned into a big-screen movie. Ricky played his soap opera character in the movie, winning a Heraldo Award – the Mexican equivalent of an Oscar – for his assured performance.

> Ricky had his first taste of life in front of the camera when he was very young.

Within weeks of his first appearance, women across the US had lost their hearts to this hunky Latin lover.

Ricky's success in Mexico helped open the door to the American television industry. In 1993, Ricky landed a role in a short-lived sitcom called *Getting By*, which starred Cindy Marshall from 1960s TV show *Laverne and Shirley*. Ricky's next acting role was in the legendary US soap opera *General Hospital*. Ricky played Miguel, a Puerto Rican musician with a troubled past. His character worked as a bartender and also sang on the show. Within weeks of his first appearance, women across the US had lost their hearts to this hunky Latin lover.

While he was in the cast of *General Hospital*, Ricky was interviewed in Miami for MTV, where he told the reporter that his biggest dream was to appear on Broadway. Richard Jay-Alexander, the producer of the acclaimed musical *Les Miserables*, saw the interview and immediately telephoned Ricky in New York to offer him the role of Marius, a young revolutionary. It was a dream come true!

To prepare for the part, Ricky went to see the musical over twenty times. He wanted his Broadway debut to be perfect! Besides the character of Marius, he also played a couple of minor parts, which meant that he was on stage for over three hours every night. He has said that although the work was very demanding, requiring a lot of self-discipline, he loved every minute of his time on Broadway.

By now, Ricky was very well known in the Latin world as an actor and a singer. Naturally he was the first choice for the title role in the Spanish-language version of Disney's *Hercules*. In addition to providing Hercules' voice, Ricky also sang the theme song, "No Importa la Distancia".

With his newfound global fame, Ricky is now being offered dozens of roles in movies and TV series. Will Ricky abandon music for the lure of the dramatic arts? Not for a while! He has said that although he would consider returning to acting somewhere down the line, right now his focus is 100 per cent on his musical career.

Chapter Five
Live for One Night Only!

Ever since his days in Menudo, Ricky Martin has been performing to huge audiences around the world. And with the huge popularity of Menudo in Latin America, and Ricky's TV fame, it hasn't been hard for him to win over audiences as a solo performer.

HIS FIRST solo tour played to packed houses everywhere – and this time it was just for him! Not wanting to rest on his laurels, however, Ricky felt he was ready to step out and introduce himself to the rest of the world.

Ricky was an instant hit in Italy and Spain, where his debut album soared high in the charts. Other parts of the world soon caught on, and it reached gold status in eight countries, mainly due to his extensive touring. The tour for his second solo album, *Me Amaras*, only built on his success, and he continued to win over throngs of newly devoted fans everywhere his plane touched down.

Due to the huge commercial success of Ricky's first two solo albums in Latin America, Ricky certainly didn't need to expand his audience for financial reasons – he just wanted to communicate with more people through his music. While touring the world he will often greet an audience in their native language, and in some cases he will perform whole songs in other languages – he's fluent in five!

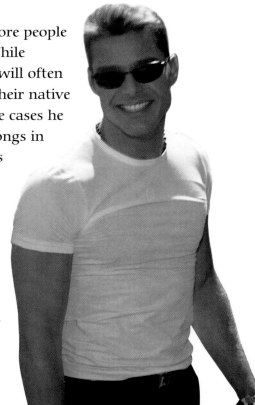

He will often greet an audience in their native language.

He puts his all – his heart and his soul, not to mention his sweat! – into every single show that he plays.

Another reason that building an international audience has been so important to Ricky is that it helps to keep his feet on the ground. He has said that it's good for him to introduce himself to a whole new audience which is unfamiliar with his music. With his new worldwide fame, it will soon be hard for him to find a new audience to cultivate!

For as long as he has been performing, both in his Menudo days and as a solo performer, Ricky has been touring the world almost non-stop. His tour schedule would make most people's heads spin, but he takes it in his stride. It's not unusual for Ricky to play shows in Asia, Europe, South America and the United States in the course of one month, criss-crossing back and forth across the globe. He has set some boundaries to maintain his sanity, however: he will only tour for fifteen days in a row, and takes breaks of four or five days in between periods on the road.

But you won't hear Ricky complain about this hectic schedule. For him, there is nothing greater or more satisfying than to bring a packed auditorium to its feet, to connect with an audience and get everyone dancing.

Ricky has said that he feels it's very important to give his all on stage, and his shows are often dazzling live spectacles. He may go through five wardrobe changes and make many dramatic entrances, using spectacular lighting effects. His show also includes dancers, live musicians and backing singers to add to the drama of the performance.

Touring has always been an important part of Ricky's career, and he has said that performing on stage is one of the most rewarding aspects of his life. He puts his all – his heart and his soul, not to mention his sweat! – into every single show that he plays. The result, Ricky says, is that if you haven't seen him perform live, then you haven't seen him at all.

As word spreads about Ricky and his incredible live shows, it is becoming harder and harder for his fans to get tickets, and his shows sell out almost instantly. As far back as 1995, when he was touring with his smash album *A Medio Vivir*, he set a new world record for the largest audience ever when he played to a house of 275,000 people in Buenos Aires, Argentina. The record had been previously held by world famous tenor Luciano Pavarotti – and before that by Menudo of course!

✻

On 11 May 1999, the day that Ricky's hugely anticipated English-language debut CD was scheduled to hit the stores,

11,000 people packed the streets and sidewalks outside Tower Records in New York City. The first fans arrived in the small hours of the morning; some had driven all night to be there. All morning and afternoon, the crowd grew. People were hanging out, dancing and chatting. The excitement was mounting.

Thousands of fans, many carrying posters and gifts, cried and screamed out Ricky's name.

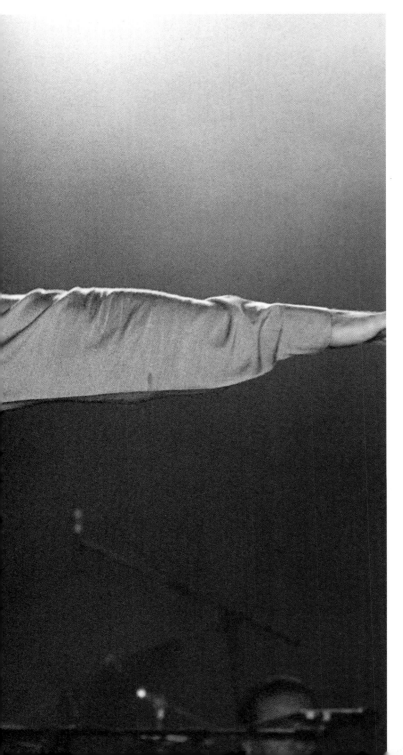

Suddenly, amid eardrum-exploding screams, shrieks and cheers, and with speakers blaring out the hottest song of the moment, a car worked its way through the throng. Ricky Martin had arrived.

The sound at Tower Records that day was deafening. Thousands of fans, many carrying posters and gifts, cried and screamed out Ricky's name. Even the star himself appeared flabbergasted by the response. He stayed and signed records for devoted fans for four hours.

Scenes like this were repeated all over America. At Tower Records in West Hollywood, California, 5,000 fans gathered for a chance to glimpse their idol. 7,000 more massed at Specs Music in Miami Beach. When he was scheduled to perform a free outdoor concert for the NBC *Today* show in New York City, the authorities provided maps of alternate routes for people who worked in the area. For that event, fans camped out overnight to guarantee a sighting of Ricky.

Ricky has been in the spotlight since he was twelve years old, but he takes it all in his stride. He has no trouble being personable with his fans and tries to make time for them whenever he can. Sometimes he even answers their e-mails, although he says that people have a hard time believing that it's really Ricky who is writing back!

One of Ricky's most endearing features is his modesty. He truly appreciates the fact that it's his fans who have made his dream of being a world-famous performer come true. While some performers might prefer to play only where they know they will sell out shows, Ricky is willing to take the risk of playing somewhere where people might not know who he is. His goal, he says, is to win them over – and he always does!

Amazed store personnel and the media couldn't help but compare Ricky to Elvis Presley, the only other male solo artist ever to have caused such frenzy. Across the country, Ricky Martin's signing appearances broke attendance records.

Well before he was a household name in North America and the UK, fans in Europe, Latin America and Asia mobbed Ricky every time he appeared. At an appearance in Puerto Rico, he had no choice but to take a helicopter to get to his own show – The 20,000 fans that showed up to greet their homeboy made driving impossible!

Sometimes he even answers their e-mails, although he says that people have a hard time believing that it's really Ricky who is writing back!

Chapter Six
The Real Ricky

Ricky Martin has it all: fame, fortune, good looks, talent, houses around the world and millions of adoring fans. But despite all this, he still loves the simple things in life, like hanging out with his friends (many of whom are the same friends he's had since childhood) washing his car, going to the beach or playing with his two dogs.

HIS LIFE is so crazy and chaotic that he needs peace and calm when he's not working. Ricky owns homes in Miami, Los Angeles, Spain and Argentina, where he can unwind and just be himself during breaks from touring. When he isn't on stage or in front of a camera, Ricky strives to be just a regular guy.

The success of Ricky the Star has everything to do with the personality of Ricky the Man. Since his early childhood he has shown remarkable stubbornness and drive. When he was initially rejected for Menudo, it only made him more determined to become a member of the group. It took three auditions, but he finally succeeded! Throughout his life, Ricky's inner strength, confidence and vision have given him the drive to achieve his goals.

Ricky is also an extremely humble guy. He knows that even though he has worked hard for all that he has, he has also been very lucky and is eternally grateful for the opportunities he has had. He chooses not to focus on the negative aspects of his experiences but on the positive ones. Ricky never expected fame to be handed to him on a silver platter, and he knows that his success is the result of careful choices and dogged determination.

When he isn't on stage or in front of a camera, Ricky strives to be just a regular guy.

Ricky hasn't always had such a sense of personal balance. During his years in Menudo he learned that he could have whatever he wanted by snapping his fingers. It was easy for a teenage boy to let fame go to his head. He had money, adulation and no responsibilities except to rehearse and perform. Everything was taken care of for him. After he left Menudo, Ricky had to learn to take care of himself and be responsible for the first time in his life. It was a time of emotional and spiritual soul-searching. Despite this struggle, Ricky credits this period as one of the best times in his life, because he had the opportunity to figure out who he was.

The fact that Ricky was estranged from his father at this

After he left Menudo, Ricky had to learn to take care of himself and be responsible.

time seems to have added to his anguish. He has recalled that he reached a crisis state just when he and his father were beginning to reconcile. Ricky came close to having a nervous breakdown, locking himself away and crying constantly. It took some time and a lot of emotional upheaval, but Ricky finally made up with his father, and learned to let himself experience peace and calm. It was the beginning of a spiritual quest that Ricky continues to pursue to this day.

Ricky's co-stars on *General Hospital* noticed the difference in Ricky's attitude immediately. Lily Melgar, the actress who played Ricky's love interest, has said that after he reconciled with his father, Ricky seemed to have found some new "inner peace".

Another turning point in Ricky's life came when he went to India in December 1998. He was exposed to elements of the Buddhist faith and began to learn yoga, which fascinated him. Today he meditates every day and often does yoga to relax before big shows.

Ricky is fiercely proud of his Puerto Rican heritage and bristles whenever anyone suggests that he is selling out by pursuing the English-language market. In interviews he loves to sing the praises of his birthplace and has even filmed a commercial to encourage people to spend their vacations there! Even though Ricky doesn't live in Puerto Rico right now, he loves to go there to visit his friends and family – and to be with "his people".

He feels so strongly about introducing people to Puerto Rican culture and breaking stereotypes about Puerto Ricans that he recently turned down the opportunity to star in a remake of *West Side Story* opposite Jennifer Lopez. For Ricky, appearing in the musical would be an endorsement of the stereotypes it portrays: that Puerto Ricans are all violent gang members. He has said that it would have been a slap in the face of the people he loves.

Ricky always encourages his fans to follow their passions and stick to their beliefs – and there's no doubt that Ricky has achieved his current success by doing just that!

Ricky always encourages his fans to follow their passions and stick to their beliefs.

Chapter Seven
Romantic Ricky

There is much more to Ricky Martin than his remarkable musical talent, as *People* magazine recognized in 1999 when it named him one of the 50 sexiest people in the world. He's still getting used to being considered one of the world's hottest sex symbols, and used to worry that it would take attention away from his music, but a conversation he had with fellow Latin star Gloria Estefan made him feel a lot more comfortable with his sexy image. If you've got it, she told him, flaunt it!

ONE THING millions of Ricky's fans want to know is whether the handsome and charming Ricky is single. Despite his high profile, Ricky likes to keep his romantic life private – he says that if he feels he has to live that part of his life in the public eye, he will give up performing for good. He has revealed, however, that he is no stranger to the pain of heartbreak, having endured a long-distance relationship which left him "eaten up" with jealousy.

Ricky admits he's a hopeless romantic who falls in love twenty times a day. Referring to his hit song "Maria", he has confessed that there was a real Maria in his life – he won't reveal her real name – and that she drove him crazy. He has also admitted to finding himself once very close to the altar. He was at the point of shopping for an engagement ring when he suddenly realized he wasn't ready for that level of commitment.

He's a hopeless romantic who falls in love twenty times a day.

For now, Ricky is happy to be single and to devote all of his time to his career.

Some people have speculated that the real Maria is Mexican television star Rebeca de Alba, the blonde beauty on his arm at the 1999 Grammy awards. Ricky first met Rebeca when he was eighteen years old, and the two have reportedly had an on-off relationship for the past ten years. Rebecca is currently living and working in Spain, and it seems their constant separation and the demands of both of their careers have taken a toll on the relationship. While hedging for a while about the status of their relationship, Ricky has definitely confirmed that he is single.

One possible reason for the split may have been Ricky's duet with Madonna, "Be Careful (Cuidado Con Mi Corazón)". It's no secret that Madonna loves Latin men, and some said Rebecca wasn't too pleased with the pairing, although Ricky insists that he and the big "M" are just friends. For now, Ricky is happy to be single and to devote all of his time to his career.

Ricky's desire for secrecy in his relationships isn't only for

selfish reasons – he also says it's a way to respect the privacy of the woman he is with. He chose this lifestyle, but he doesn't want to impose it on anyone else he loves.

While the attention he receives as a sex symbol hasn't lessened since his days with Menudo, Ricky's attitude to it has changed as he has matured. Now he looks forward to one day being a faithful husband and loving father. He grew up in a large, loving family, and has said he admires the large, tight-knit families he sees in his travels.

Whoever Ricky chooses to spend his life with when he does decide to settle down, she's going to have to be patient, because right now everything and everyone else has to take a back seat to the biggest priority in Ricky's life: his musical career. The months he spends on the road make Ricky's dream of a normal family life almost impossible, and he has said he doesn't feel he can provide a woman with the stable life that she deserves at the moment.

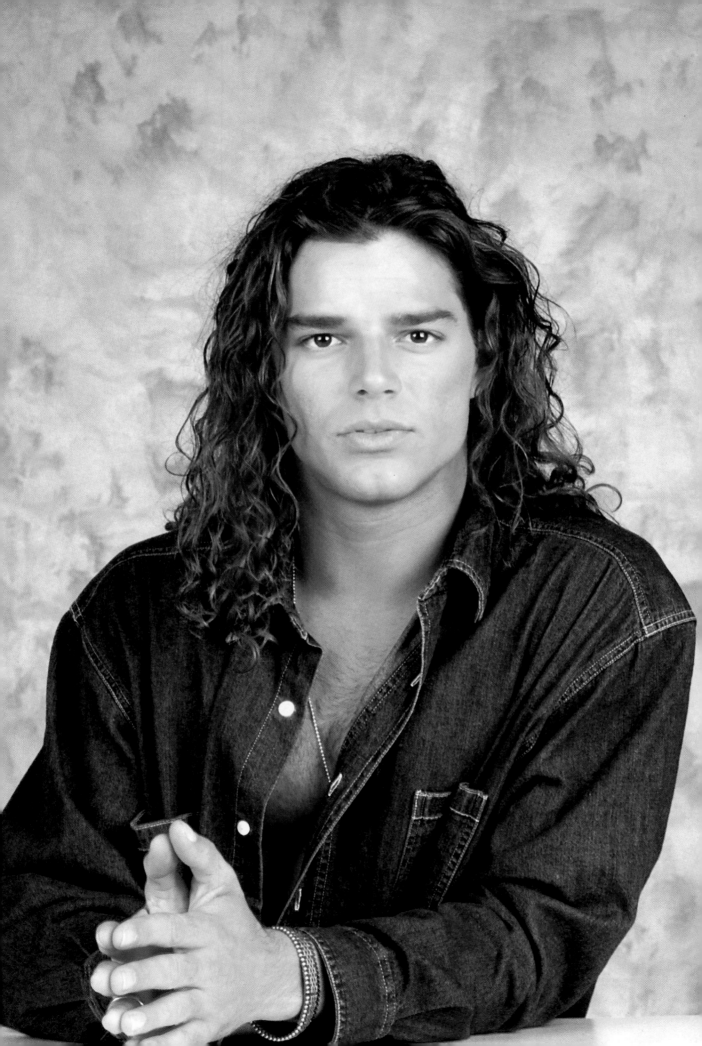

When the time comes, there are definitely some things Ricky will look for in Ms Right. For one thing, she will have to be spiritual. Ricky credits his spiritual life with keeping him grounded during the ups and downs of his career. She will have to enjoy tropical places as well because that's where Ricky likes to spend his free time. Key West in Florida, Spain and Brazil top his list of ideal holiday spots.

A spontaneous sense of adventure is also the key to Ricky's heart. Once while touring in Argentina he had himself rolled up in a blanket like a burrito to escape the huge crowd waiting outside his hotel room. He and his friends took a cab to a small tango bar, where they had an impromptu jam session with the proprietor and another patron. He claims that it was the best concert he's ever given!

Nonetheless, Ricky's girl shouldn't be too much of a party animal. Drugs and drinking are out of the question – Ricky doesn't even drink wine. The calm and peaceful life that is so important to Ricky right now can only be achieved with a clear head.

He thinks a woman's sexiest features are her legs.

Ricky has his intellectual side too – French author Victor Hugo is a hero of his, and he also admires the Columbian writer Gabriel Garcia Marquez. Ricky's girl has to be intelligent, but there are also certain physical features that Ricky looks for in a woman. Beautiful skin and big eyes rate highly with him, and he thinks a woman's sexiest features are her legs. He's partial to Latin women because of their shared culture, but any woman who can cook him an authentic Puerto Rican meal has certainly found the way to Ricky's heart.

With his career taking the front seat right now, only time will tell which lucky woman has what it takes to make Ricky happy in the future.

Chapter Eight
Ricky Facts

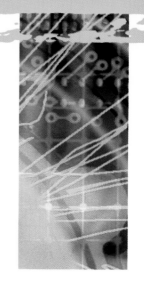

- ☀ Ricky's most cherished childhood memory is his first aeroplane ride. He was going to Orlando, Florida to visit Disney World.
- ☀ Ricky has a tattoo of a flower in a "personal" location!
- ☀ The guests at Ricky's ultimate dinner party would be Gandhi, Nelson Mandela, Einstein, the Dalai Lama and the Pope. He would serve them Puerto Rican food!
- ☀ Ricky surfs the Internet with his Mac laptop.
- ☀ Growing up, Ricky was an altar boy at his church.
- ☀ Even though he was raised on an island whose staple food was fish, Ricky can't stand seafood!
- ☀ In Brazil, Menudo were once the most popular recording act of all time – surpassing even Julio Iglesias and Michael Jackson.
- ☀ Ricky's grandmother was a writer who published four books.
- ☀ He wears a size eleven shoe.
- ☀ The best gift you can give Ricky is incense. He loves it!
- ☀ Ricky's astrological sign is Capricorn. According to Chinese astrology, he was born in the Year of the Pig.
- ☀ Ricky's biggest fear is snakes.

❈ Ricky can't keep his hands off junk food!

❈ Adventuresome Ricky's number one outdoor activity is skydiving.

❈ If Ricky wasn't a performer he's said he'd like to have been a school psychologist or a doctor – but he's said he'd probably be flipping burgers and going door-to-door begging for the opportunity to sing!

❈ Ricky's most embarrassing moment came when he slipped on a rose someone had thrown on the stage. He pretended that his odd movements were all part of the act!

❈ As an actor, Ricky dreams of working with Al Pacino or Harvey Keitel.

❈ Ricky plans to spend New Year's Eve 1999 in a tent in the Himalayas.

❈ If he were stranded on a desert island, Ricky would like to have music, a hammock and some incense.

❈ Ricky has two dogs: A Golden Retriever named Icara and a Chihuahua named Titan.

❈ Ricky once strode down the catwalk as a model for Giorgio Armani.

❈ Ricky had an audience with and was blessed by Pope John Paul II.

❈ Ricky once performed in four countries in one day – the inspiration for the song "Livin' La Vida Loca".

Chapter Nine
Looking Towards Tomorrow

At rock legend Sting's annual rainforest benefit concert at New York's legendary Carnegie Hall in the spring of 1999, Ricky Martin delighted the crowd by performing the Frank Sinatra standard, "I've Got the World on a String". With Ricky-mania going full throttle, the song couldn't have been more appropriate. But with all of his dreams of success as a performer coming true, what more can the future hold for this multi-talented star?

NOT SURPRISINGLY given his matinee-idol looks and proven acting skill, the big screen has been beckoning. He has said that he regularly receives film scripts including, he admits, some very juicy roles. But for Ricky the movies can wait. He is adamant that his music career is going to remain his number one priority for the time being. Down the line, however – perhaps in five years' time – he's said he might just take those offers more seriously. Ricky's not just interested in acting, either; he's said he'd like to branch out into writing and directing if he gets the opportunity.

Given his matinee-idol looks and proven acting skill, the big screen has been beckoning.

Even within the musical spectrum, the possibilities for Ricky seem endless. He has promised his legions of fans that he will not stop recording in Spanish, so don't be surprised if you hear that another Spanish-language album is on the way soon. And in typical Ricky Martin fashion, he's not interested in limiting himself to one facet of the music business – he may try his hand at directing videos or even producing other musicians.

With the opening of his restaurant Casa Salsa in Miami Beach in late 1998, Ricky has introduced another side of his personality: Ricky the businessman and entrepreneur. He got the idea to open Casa Salsa when he became homesick for the delicious regional cooking of his native island. To keep things authentic, he even imported the chef from his favorite hometown restaurant in San Juan!

When it comes down to what to do next, ambitious Ricky hasn't ruled out one surprising option – medical school! He's always been a frustrated doctor, he says, and loves the idea of helping people with their problems. If the idea of Dr Ricky Martin seems far-fetched, think again. For someone with such a strong track record of achieving his dreams, nothing is impossible!

Chart-topper, movie star, restaurateur, family man… Which direction will the multi-talented Ricky take next?

He's not interested in limiting himself to one facet of the music business – he may try his hand at directing videos or even producing other musicians.

Album Discography

RICKY MARTIN   487372 (Sony Discos)

Fuego Contra Fuego/Dime Que Me Quires/
Corazon Entre Nubes/Ser Feliz/Susana/
Conmigo Nadie Puede/Vuelo/El Amor De
Mi Vida/Te Voy A Conquistar/Popotitos/
Juego De Ajedrez

ME AMARAS   474335 (Sony Discos)

No Me Pidas Mas/Es Mejor Decirse Adios/
Entre El Amor Y Los Halagos/Lo Que Nos
Pase, Pasara/Ella Es/Me Amaras/Ayudame/
Eres Como El Aire/Que Dia Es Hoy (Self
Control)/Hooray! Hooray! It's a Holi-
Holiday

A MEDIO VIVIR   489160 (Sony Discos)

Fuego De Noche, Nieve De Dia/A Medio
Vivir/Maria/Te Extraño, Te Olvido, Te Amo/
Donde Estaras/Volveras/Revolucion/ Somos
La Semilla/Como Decirte Adios/ Bombon
De Azucar/Corazon/Nada Es Imposible

VUELVE   488789 (Sony Discos)

Por Arriba, Por Abajo/Lola, Lola/Casi Un
Bolero/Corazonado/La Bomba/Vuelve/
Hagamos El Amor/La Copa De La Vida/
Perdido Sin Ti/Asi Es La Vida/Marcia Baila/
No Importa La Distancia/Gracias Por Pensa
En Mi/La Copa De La Vida - The Cup Of
Life (Spanglish Radio Edit)

RICKY MARTIN   494406
(Sony/Columbia - Europe)
CK 69891
(Sony/Columbia - USA)

Livin' La Vida Loca/Spanish Eyes/She's All
I Ever Had/Shake Your Bon-Bon/Be Careful
(Cuidado Con Mi Corazón) (with
Madonna)/I Am Made Of You/Love You For
A Day/Private Emotion (with Meja)/The
Cup Of Life (Spanglish Radio Edit)/You
Stay With Me/Livin' La Vida Loca (Spanish
version)/I Count The Minutes/Bella (She's
All I Ever Had)/Maria (Spanglish Radio
Edit)

Picture Acknowledgements

All Action
12, 17, 23, 33, 61
R. Corlouer 2, 8, 56, 57
Paul Smith 25

Colorific
Nat Bocking/Shooting Star 58
Ron Davis/Shooting Star 14, 26,
29, 36, 55
Danny Feld/Shooting Star 13
Barry King/Shooting Star 1, 10,
16, 47, 50, 51
Gary Marshall/Shooting Star 3,
37, 39, 43

Lisa O'Connor/Shooting Star 45
George Rodriguez/Shooting Star
52

Corbis
Mitch Gerber 11, 28, 31, 38, 42
Robert Milazzo 7, 53
Neal Preston 15, 24, 48, 49

Redferns
JM International 27

Rex Features
Krueger 9, 30, 62

Camilla Morandi 4, 22
Erik Pendzich 35
Brian Rasic 6, 32, 44, 54
Leon Schadeberg 40

South Beach Photo Agency
63
Giancarlo Johansson 34, 60
Pablo Grosby 46

Starfile
Vinnie Zuffante 18, 19, 20, 21